INSPIRATIONS

OF

THE HEART

THROUGH

SCRIPTURES

INSPIRATIONS
OF
THE HEART

THROUGH SCRIPTURES

JACQUI J.

Foreword

Inspirations of the Heart through Scriptures provides a heartfelt opportunity to read God's word, be inspired and experience a reflective thought on how God's word can apply and inspire you.

Let's journey into a world of inspirational scriptures as a reminder of how God's words can inspire you and remind you of how he loves you.

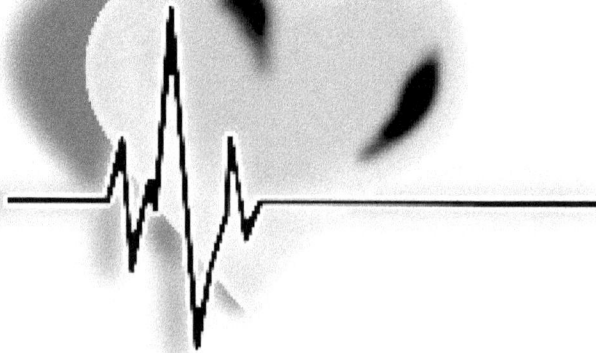

Inspirations of the Heart through Scriptures

Acknowledgements

This book is dedicated to my young ladies (Latoria L. Johnson and Amber T.N. Johnson) and my one and only grandson (Cari D. Perkins). They inspire me daily.

My desire to write this book and inspire others stem from my relationship with God – for he is the center of my joy, the light of my life, the breath I breathe and my very pulse. It is because of God's love that I am. Thus I seek to give back all he has given me to glorify him. Praise his HOLY NAME.

Table of Content

INSPIRATIONS
OF
THE HEART

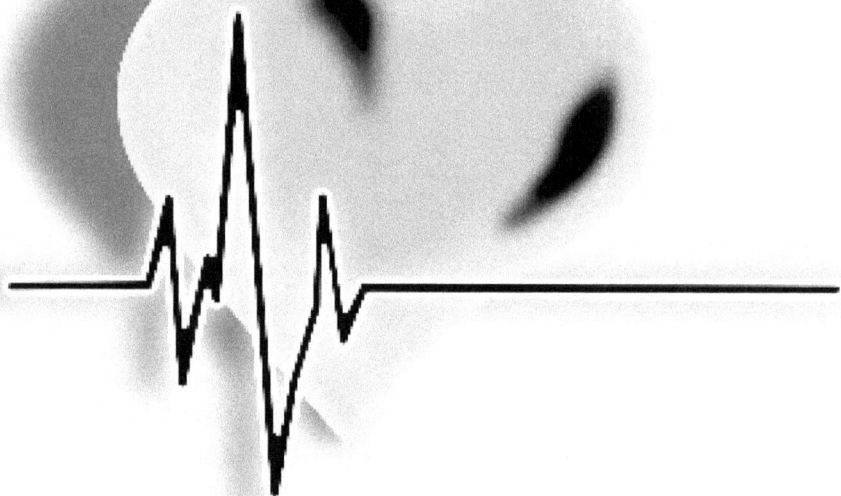

THROUGH SCRIPTURES

ACCEPTANCE

Acceptance is something that many yearn to receive from others. Just believing and knowing that God accepts you just as you are. He designed you just the way he wants you to be. Think not about whether people accept you and know that God accepted you before you existed.

1 Timothy 4:9
This is a trustworthy saying that deserves full acceptance.

Romans 11:15
For if their rejection brought reconciliation to the world, what will their acceptance be but life from the dead?

Romans 15:7
Accept one another, then, just as Christ accepted you, in order to bring praise to God.

John 6:37
All those the Father gives me will come to me, and whoever comes to me I will never drive away.

REFLECTION: *What did the scriptures tell you about* ***acceptance*** *and how can you apply these scriptures to knowing that* ***acceptance*** *is something God has already infused in your life?*

_____

_____

_____

_____

Which scripture(s) spoke to you and inspired you regarding ***acceptance*** *in your life and why?*

_____

_____

_____

_____

*Why did the scripture(s) inspire or speak to you and how can you use them as a reminder that you are **accepted** by God?*

_____

_____

_____

_____

_____

ADMIRATION

There is admiration in knowing that when you have respect and approval, you can feel a sense of love. That is the kind of feeling you can receive when you have admiration of God. A sense of belonging, power and love.

Psalms 139:14
I praise you because I am fearfully and wonderfully made; your works are wonderful, I know that full well.

Ephesians 3:18
May have power, together with all the Lord's holy people, to grasp how wide and long and high and deep is the love of Christ,

Philippians 3:14
I press on toward the goal to win the prize for which God has called me heavenward in Christ Jesus.

Philippians 4:8
Finally, brothers and sisters, whatever is true, whatever is noble, whatever is right, whatever is pure, whatever is lovely, whatever is admirable – if anything is excellent or praiseworthy – think about such things.

*REFLECTION: What did the scriptures reveal to you about **admiration**?*

_____

_____

_____

_____

_____

*Which scripture(s) spoke to you regarding **admiration** at this point in your life and why?*

_____

_____

_____

_____

_____

*Why did the scripture(s) inspire you and how can you use these scriptures to maintain **admiration** for God in your life?*

_____

_____

_____

_____

_____

BEAUTY

Beauty is that which God has designed within you. He has given you so many qualities through many forms that demonstrate his love especially in his sight. Take a moment and just see the multitude of beauty around you. The beauty you see is found in many shapes, colors and forms. That's right, beauty is all around you and naturally planted inside of you.

Psalms 50:2
From Zion, perfect in beauty, God shines forth.

Isaiah 33:17
Your eyes will see the king in his beauty and view a land that stretches afar.

Psalms 27:4
One thing I ask from the Lord, this only do I seek: that I may dwell in the house of the Lord all the days of my life, to gaze on the beauty of the Lord and to seek him in his temple.

Psalms 139:14
I praise you because I am fearfully and wonderfully made; your works are wonderful, I know that full well.

*REFLECTION: What did God's word reveal to you about **beauty**?*

_____

_____

_____

_____

_____

*Which scripture(s) spoke to you regarding your **beauty** and the **beauty** inside you?*

_____

_____

_____

_____

*List ways God has planted and created **beauty** in you?*

_____

_____

_____

_____

_____

BLESSINGS

God's blessings are found in his favor and protection. He gives to each of us knowingly and unknowingly through his unconditional love for us. So, count your blessings one by one.

Psalms 128:2
You will eat the fruit of your labor; blessings and prosperity will be yours.

Deuteronomy 28:2
All these blessings will come on you and accompany you if you obey the Lord your God:

Romans 15:29
I know that when I come to you, I will come in the full measure of the blessing of Christ.

Genesis 12:2
"I will make you into a great nation, and I will bless you; I will make your name great, and you will be a blessing.

REFLECTION: *What did God's word tell you about the* **blessings** *he gives so freely?*

_____

_____

_____

_____

_____

*Which scripture(s) demonstrate God's **blessings** and what were some **blessings** you have experienced through God's love?*

_____

_____

_____

_____

_____

*Reflect on your life and all the **blessings** you have received. Share your **blessings** (one by one).*

_____

_____

_____

_____

CHARACTER

The great qualities distinctively given to us by God are amazing. What amazing gifts God has given intentionally and freely to his people! Your **character** is a direct reflection of your relationship with God,

Roman 5:4
Perseverance, character, and character, hope.

1 Corinthians 15:33
Do not be misled, "Bad company corrupts good character."

Ephesians 2:10
For we are God's handiwork, created in Christ Jesus to do good works, which God prepared in advance for us to do.

Matthew 11:29
Take my yoke upon you and learn from me, for I am gentle and humble in heart, and you will find rest for your souls.

REFLECTION: *What did you discover about having* ***character*** *as it is written in the scriptures?*

_____

_____

_____

_____

Which scripture helps to understand the importance of maintaining a God like ***character*** *in you?*

_____

_____

_____

_____

*How can you apply God's word to building or maintaining the **character** in you?*

_____

_____

_____

_____

_____

CHRISTIANITY

Christiainity often looks at a religion based quality or character in Christians. The teaching of God's word helps to build your relationship with God and develop practices that will draw you closer to understanding God's will for your life.

2 Chronicles 7:14
If my people, who are called by name, will humble Themselves and pray and seek my face and turn from their wicked ways, then I will hear from heaven, and I will forgive their sin and will heal their land.

Hebrews 13:5
Keep your lives free from the love of money and be content With what you have, because God has said, "Never will I leave you; never will I forsake you."

Matthew 5:16
In the same way, let your light shine before Others, that they may see your good Deeds and glorify your Father in heaven.

Romans 12:2

Do not conform to the pattern of this world,
But be transformed by the renewing of
Your mind. Then you will be able to test
And approve what God's will is – his good,
Pleasing and perfect will.

REFLECTION: *What did the scriptures reveal to you about* **christianity?**

_____

_____

_____

_____

Which scripture(s) stood out to you about how you can increase your **christianity?**

_____

_____

_____

_____

_____

How can you use the scripture(s) to increase your relationship with God?

_____

_____

_____

_____

_____

DEVOTION

Devotion is your level of commitment to building a relationship with God. Spending time with God are such precious moments. When you are devoting your time to God, you are increasing your faith and relationship with him. What a blessing!

1 Thessalonians 3:10
Night and day we pray most earnestly that we may see You again and supply what is lacking in your faith.

Psalms 5: 3
In the morning, Lord, you hear my voice;
In the morning I lay my requests before
You and wait expectantly.

Romans 12:10
Be devoted to one another in love.
Honor one another above yourselves.

Mark 1:35
Very early in the morning, while it was still
Dark, Jesus got up, left the house
And went off to a solitary place, where he prayed.

REFLECTION: *What did the scriptures share with you about **devotion**?*

_____

_____

_____

_____

*Which scripture(s) spoke to you regarding **devotion** and how you can apply it to your life.*

_____

_____

_____

_____

*How did the scripture(s) inspire you to set aside time(s) of **devotion** with God?*

_____

_____

_____

_____

_____

ENDURANCE

The power to have without giving up or giving way to what can be very difficult or unpleasant is endurance. Just imagine the endurance you are able to receive because of God's grace. He will give you all the power to endure, run the race and complete the course. There is power in endurance.

Colossians 1:11
Being strengthened with all power according to his glorious might so that you may have great endurance and patience.

1 Timothy 6:11
But you, man of God, flee from all this, And pursue righteousness, godliness, Faith, love, endurance and gentleness.

2 Timothy 3:10
You, however, know all about my teaching, My way of life, my purpose, Faith, patience, love, endurance,

Roman 15:5
May the God who gives endurance And encouragement give you the Same attitude of mind toward Each other that Christ Jesus had.

REFLECTION: *What did the scriptures tell you about having and maintaining **endurance**?*

_____

_____

_____

_____

_____

*Which scripture(s) spoke to you and how can you practice **endurance** in your spiritual life?*

_____

_____

_____

_____

*Reflect on a time when you needed to practice **endurance**. How did you feel and what helped you to get through the situation?*

_____

_____

_____

_____

_____

FAITH

Faith involves those moments of complete trust and that confidence in something or someone. Having that kind of faith in God is found in all that you cannot see but faith that knows that it is.

Hebrews 11:1
Now faith is confidence in what
We hope for and assurance
About what we do not see.

Hebrew 11:3
By faith we understand that the universe was
Formed at God's command, so that what
Is seen was not made out of what was
Visible.

Ephesians 2:8
For it is by grace you have been saved,
Through faith – and this is not
From yourselves, it is
The gift of God,

Hebrews 11:6
And without faith it is
Impossible to please God,
Because anyone who comes to
Him must believe that he exists
And that he rewards those
Who earnestly seeks him.

REFLECTION: *What did the scriptures reveal to you about* ***faith***?

_____

_____

_____

_____

Reflect on a time when you needed to have ***faith***. *What did you do and how were you able to apply your* ***faith***?

_____

_____

_____

_____

_____

*How can your **faith** increase and what will you do to increase **faith**?*

_____

_____

_____

_____

_____

FEAR

Fear is an unpleasant emotion that someone can have. It can be that of danger or even painful. Just know God never gave us a spirit of fear. He is all knowing and will never leave nor forsake you.

2 Timothy 1:7

For the Spirit God gave us does not make us timid, But gives us power, love and self-discipline.

Philippians 4:6

Do not be anxious about anything, but in Every situation, by prayer and petition, with Thanksgiving, present your request to God.

Philippians 4:7

And the peace of God, which transcends All understanding, will guard your hearts And your minds in Christ Jesus.

Psalm 56:3

When I am afraid, I put my trust in you.

REFLECTION: *What did the scriptures tell you about fear?*

_____

_____

_____

_____

_____

Reflect on a time when you felt **fear.** *What did you do to overcome that* **fear?**

_____

_____

_____

_____

_____

*Reflecting on any moments of **fear**, what do you think kept you from harm and danger?*

_____

_____

_____

_____

_____

FORGIVENESS

Forgiveness is that action where you are releasing and letting something go. What a great feeling that God has forgiven us and still blesses us. Just know that when forgiving others, God also forgives you.

Luke 17:4
Even if they sin against you seven times in a
Day and seven times come back to your
Saying "I repent

Ephesians 4:32
Be kind and compassionate to one another,
Forgiving each other, just as in

Matthew 6:4
For if you forgive other people when they
sin against you, your heavenly
Father will also forgive you,

Colossians 3:13
Bear with each other and forgive
One another if any of you
Jas a grievance against someone
Forgive as the Lord forgave you.

REFLECTION: *What did the scriptures tell you about* *forgiveness?*

_____

_____

_____

_____

*How can you use God's word to remind you of the kind of **forgiveness** he wants you to have towards one to another?*

_____

_____

_____

_____

*Why is **forgiveness** important and what does it mean for you?*

_____

_____

_____

_____

_____

GUIDANCE

Guidance is the advice or information meant to provide an opportunity to resolve a challenge or problem. How amazing it is that you can seek and find guidance from God who is all knowing and is the author and finisher of our faith.

Proverbs 11:14
For lack of guidance a nation falls, but
Victory is won through many advisers.

Proverbs 1:5
Let the wise listen and add to their learning,
And let the discerning get guidance –

Psalms 37:4
Take delight in the Lord, and he
Will give you the desires of your heart.

Psalms 25:5
Guide me in your truth and teach me, for
You are God my savior, and my hope is in
You all day long.

REFLECTION: *What did the scripture reveal about* ***guidance?***

_____

_____

_____

_____

_____

Have you ever had a time when you were in need of ***guidance?*** *What did you do to find the* ***guidance*** *you needed?*

_____

_____

_____

_____

*How can the scriptures help you to find **guidance** in a time of need?*

_____

_____

_____

_____

_____

*Reflect on times when you needed **guidance**. What things help you to find the **guidance** you needed in that situation?*

_____

_____

_____

_____

HOPE

The feeling of something happening and a desire for specific things to happen is hope. Understanding that hope is that feeling of trust. Seeking to trust the Lord with all your heart with all your heart and soul is an amazing hope to have.

Jeremiah 29:11
For I know the plans I have for you,"
Declares the Lord, " plans to prosper you and
Not to harm you, plans to give you
Hope and a future.

Romans 15:13
May the God of hope fill you with all joy
And peace as you trust in him, so that
You may overflow with hope by the
Power of the Holy Spirit.

Romans 15:13
May the God of hope fill you with all joy and
Peace as you trust in him, so that
You may overflow with hope by the
Power of the Holy Spirit.

Romans 12:12
Be joyful in hope, patient in affliction , faithful in prayer.

REFLECTION: *What did the scriptures reveal to you about **hope**?*

_____

_____

_____

_____

_____

*Reflect on a time when you needed to have **hope**. What feeling did you have and what did you do to gain **hope**?*

_____

_____

_____

_____

_____

*What do you think can help you to find **hope?***

_____

_____

_____

_____

_____

*List ways you can find and maintain **hope.** Did those ways work for you in the past? Why or why not?*

_____

_____

_____

_____

Joy

The feeling of happiness that is found in joy. What a pleasure it is to find joy in the love of the Lord. There is thankfulness in knowing that the spirit of the Lord provides love, joy and so much more.

James 1:2
Consider it pure joy, my brothers and sisters,
Whenever you face trials of many kinds,

Galatians 5:22
But the fruit of the Spirit is love, joy, peace, forbearance,
Kindness, goodness, faithfulness,

Luke 2:10
But the angel said to them, "Do not be
Afraid. I bring you good news that
Will cause great joy for the people.

Hebrews 12:2
Fixing our eyes on Jesus, the pioneer and
Perfecter of faith. For the joy set before him he endured
The cross, scorning its shame, and sat down at
The right hand of the throne of God.

REFLECTION: *What did the scriptures reveal to you about **joy**?*

_____

_____

_____

_____

_____

*Think about a time when you experienced **joy**. What kind of things bring you **joy**?*

_____

_____

_____

_____

_____

Have you ever had a time when you were hoping for
***joy?** Explain what you did to find the **joy** you were*
looking for?

_____

_____

_____

_____

*How can you use God's word to find and maintain **joy?***

_____

_____

_____

_____

LONELINESS

The feeling of sadness and feeling without friends or company can be all too familiar reminders of loneliness. Loneliness has no place in God's kingdom because God promises to never leave nor forsake you. He is always with you and you have a friend in him.

Matthew 28:20

And teaching them to obey everything I have commanded you. And surely I am with you always, to the very end of age."

Isaiah 41:10

So do not fear, for I am with you; do not be dismayed, for I am your God. I will strengthen you and help you; I will uphold you with my righteous right hand.

Psalm 23:4

Even though I walk through the darkest valley, I will fear no evil, for you are with me; your rod and your staff, they comfort me.

1 Peter 5:7
Cast all your anxiety on him because he cares for you.

REFLECTION: *According to the scriptures, what is revealed about* **loneliness?**

_____

_____

_____

_____

Can you recall a time in your life when you felt **lonely**? *How did you overcome that feeling?*

_____

_____

_____

_____

*How can you apply God's word to **loneliness?***

_____

_____

_____

_____

_____

LOVE

Love such a precious gift. So unconditional and so true. So pure and so powerful. So amazing and yet so rare. Experiencing love is what we all long to do. Having the love of God is something we all have unconditionally.

John 3:16

For God so loved the world that he gave his one and only Son, that whoever believes in him shall not perish but have eternal life.

Romans 5:8

But God demonstrates his own love for us in this: While we were still sinners, Christ died for us.

1 Corinthians 13:4-5

Love is patient, love is kind. It does not envy, it does not boast, it is not proud. It does not dishonor others, it is not self-seeking, it is not easily angered, it keeps no record of wrongs.

1 Corinthians 13:6-7

Love does not delight in evil but rejoice with the truth. 7) it always protects, always trusts, always hopes, always perseveres.

REFLECTION: *What did the scriptures reveal to you about* **love***?*

_____

_____

_____

_____

_____

What does **love** *mean to you?*

_____

_____

_____

_____

_____

*How can you apply the scriptures to help you to experience a God kind of **love**?*

_____

_____

_____

_____

*Reflect on a time when you felt **love**. Was it the kind of **love** God gives so freely to us? Why or why not?*

_____

_____

_____

_____

OBEDIENCE

The art of obedience can be hard to do. Being obedient to God brings about a level of truth. Compliance in order, through request you must stay along with something that can last. Scripture reminds us that surrendering to God's will and casting cares brings. OBEDIENCE!

Deuteronomy 8:6

Observe the commands of the Lord your God, walking in obedience to him and revering him.

Psalms 128:1

Blessed are all who fear the Lord, who walk in obedience to him.

Hebrews 5:8

Son though he was, he learned obedience from what he suffered.

Philemon 1:21

Confident of your obedience, I write to you, knowing that you will do even more than I ask.

REFLECTION: *What did the scriptures reveal to you about **obedience**?*

_____

_____

_____

_____

*Can you recall a time when you were not **obedient**? What happened and what was the result of your disobedience?*

_____

_____

_____

_____

_____

*How can you apply God's word to help you to remember to be **obedient**?*

_____

_____

_____

_____

STRENGTH

There is power in strength. Imagine that inner strength that lies within. With practice through time your strength will increase. Just discover what you will build from an increased strength from thee. Having faith and trust in God is the strength I take joy in receiving

from that which is HE.

Philippians 4:13

I can do all this through him who gives me strength.

2 Corinthians 12:9

But he said to me, "My grace is sufficient for you, for my power is made perfect in weakness." Therefore I will boast all the more gladly about my weaknesses, so that Christ's power may rest on me.

Isaiah 40:29

He gives strength to the weary and increases the power of the weak.

Isaiah 40:31

But those who hope in the Lord will renew their strength. They will soar on wings like eagles; they will run and not grow weary, they will walk and not be faint.

REFLECTION: *What did the scriptures reveal to you about* **strength**?

_____

_____

_____

_____

_____

What does **strength** *mean to you and why do you need* **strength**?

_____

_____

_____

_____

_____

*How can you apply God's word to gaining **strength**?*

_____

_____

_____

_____

*When you are weak how can you gain **strength**?*

_____

_____

_____

_____

TRUST

When you trust, there is an opportunity for you to believe in something. Something that you can rely on. How amazing to know that you can always trust in God, He will never leave nor forsake you. Just know you can always place your trust in HIM.

Proverbs 3:5,6

Trust in the Lord with all your heart and lean not on your own understanding. 6) in all yours ways submit to him, and he will make your paths straight.

Philippians 4:6

Do not be anxious about anything, but in every situation, by prayer and petition, with thanksgiving, present your requests to God.

Romans 8:28

And we know that in all things God works for the good of those who love him, who have been called according to his purpose.

Psalms 56:3

When I am afraid, I put my trust in you.

REFLECTION: *What did the scriptures reveal about* ***trust?***

_____

_____

_____

_____

_____

Reflect on a time when you needed to ***trust*** *something or someone. How did you feel?*

_____

_____

_____

_____

_____

What did you do to either build your trust or overcome your lack of ***trust?***

_____

_____

_____

_____

_____

*How can you apply God's word to establish **trust**?*

_____

_____

_____

_____

_____

TRIALS

Trials can be a test of something. Through trials comes growth, experiences sometimes challenging. The great news is that trials won't last always.

James 1:2

Consider it pure, joy, my brothers and sisters, whenever you face trials of many kinds,

Deuteronomy 29:3

With your own eyes you saw those great trials, those signs and great wonders.

Luke 22:28

You are those who have stood by me in my trials.

James 1:12

Blessed is the one who perseveres under trial because, having stood the test, that person will receive the crown of life that the Lord has promised to those who love him.

REFLECTION: *What did the scriptures reveal about* **trials?**

_____

_____

_____

_____

_____

Can you recall a time when you experienced some **trials?** *What did that feel like?*

_____

_____

_____

_____

_____

How did you overcome your **trial(s)?**

_____

_____

_____

_____

_____

_____

How can you use God's word to help you with any **trial(s)?**

_____

_____

_____

_____

TRIUMPHS

Praise be to God for life's triumphs. Those great victories and achievements that come in this life. Giving victory beyond any of life's downfalls. For the Lord is with you and helps you to triumph over any negatives.

Psalms 118:7

The Lord is with me; he is my helper, I look in triumph on my enemies.

Psalms 25:2

I trust in you; do not let me be put to shame, nor let my enemies triumph over me.

Psalms 41:11

I know that you are pleased with me, for my enemy does not triumph over me.

Job 17:4

You have closed their minds to understanding; therefore you will not let them triumph.

REFLECTION: *What did the scriptures reveal about* **triumph?**

_____

_____

_____

_____

Reflect on a time when you experienced **triumph***. What was that experience?*

_____

_____

_____

_____

How did that **triumph** *make you feel?*

_____

How can you apply God's word to that **triumph**?

WISDOM

There is greatness in knowledge when wisdom is present. It's that trust and the consideration with care of that which will change a course. It is the application of wisdom that drives informed decision making.

James 1:5

If any of you lacks wisdom, you should ask God, who gives generously to all without finding fault, and it will be given to you.

Proverbs 1:7

The fear of the Lord is the beginning of knowledge, but fools despise wisdom and instruction.

Proverbs 2:6

For the Lord gives wisdom; from his mouth come knowledge and understanding.

James 3:17

But the wisdom that comes from heaven is first of all pure; then peace-loving, considerate, submissive, full of mercy and good fruit, impartial and sincere.

REFLECTION: *What did the scriptures reveal about* **wisdom?**

_____

_____

_____

_____

_____

What does it mean to have and use **wisdom?**

_____

_____

_____

_____

_____

Reflect on your use of wisdom. List ways in which you use **wisdom** *in your life.*

_____

_____

_____

_____

_____

How can you use God's word to increase your use of ***wisdom?***

_____

_____

_____

_____

Inspiration of the Heart Through Scriptures

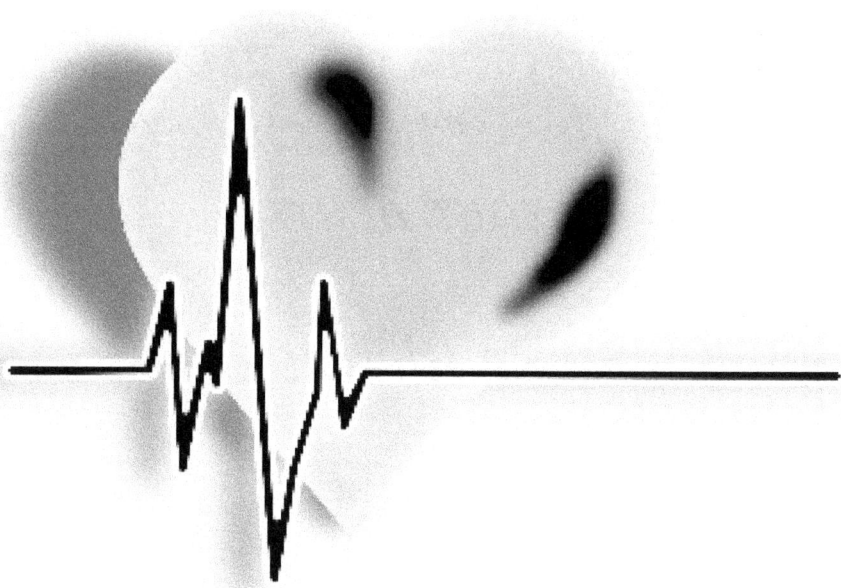

REFLECTIVE THOUGHTS

It is my hope that you as the reader obtained inspiration from God's word. May your heart be inspired and your soul be fed.

For this book was an inspiration of the heart meant to inspire and bless your heart!

Be Blessed!

Check out other books from Jacqui J.

The ABCs of Spiritual Living

(Currently on Amazon)

Coming Soon

Inspirations of the Heart
Book of Poetry

SEAP
into becoming a better you

Declaring to SEAP
Daily devotional
Guide to a better you

RESET
A time to relax, reflect, release and reflect

"49" Ways of Forgiveness

FAITH UNDER FIRE
A Time to Believe

Resources

www.ingramcontent.com/pod-product-compliance
Lightning Source LLC
Chambersburg PA
CBHW071239090426
42736CB00014B/3149